In a Long Day

The Titshall photographs of farm and village life

SELECTED BY DAVID KINDRED
Captions by Roger Smith

First published 1999

British Library Cataloguing in Publication Data
A catalogue record for this book is available from the British Library.

ISBN 0 9533651 5 8

Published by

Old Pond Publishing
104 Valley Road
Ipswich
IP1 4PA

Phone/fax 01473 210176

Cover design and book layout by Liz Whatling.
Origination by Reflex Reprographics.
Printed in Great Britain by Ebenezer Baylis, Worcester.

Contents

Jack Amos, born in Kirton, Suffolk in 1903, who shepherded at Bucklesham and Kirton. He had probably been using his hoe to chop out turnips for the ewes, and at his feet is a billhook of East Anglian design. Jack lived until Christmas 1997.

INTRODUCTION

A kind-faced elderly gentleman came to me one day with a six-word question, "Are you interested in old photographs?" This turned out to be a very important enquiry, one that was to lead me to thousands of hours of very interesting and enjoyable work.

The man was Doug Cotton who had seen some of the vintage photographs I had gathered and published in the Ipswich *Evening Star* where I am picture editor. He told me in his wonderful broad Suffolk accent that he had several hundred large glass negatives that he had stored in his loft since the 1950s. Born in 1912, Doug was brought up in the country, working with his father Harry as threshing machine contractors. By the age of fifteen, when they were busy, Doug was in charge, driving a threshing machine and elevator with a steam engine.

Ralph Titshall

At about this time he got to know a photographer, Ralph Titshall, through a joint interest in beekeeping. In the nineteenth century members of the Titshall family were millers in Suffolk; Ralph and his brother Leonard were born at the turn of the century, two of eleven children. From 1924 they ran a photographer's business from 436 Spring Road, Ipswich, a house built by one of their elder brothers. It appears that while Ralph was essentially the studio photographer and the one who did the developing and printing, Leonard travelled around Ipswich and the surrounding countryside looking for commissions, using a motorbike and sidecar to transport his large box camera and tripod. Leonard left Titshall Bros in 1947, and indeed Doug Cotton remembers seeing very little of him.

Ralph ran the business until 1968 when the house was sold, to become an antiques shop and more recently a private residence. The present owners have restored the roof of the wooden portrait studio which still stands in the yard with some of its original fittings.

Doug remembers Ralph as slightly eccentric, dressed in thick tweed, knickerbocker trousers, buskins and a 'John Tricker' (narrow-brimmed trilby) hat. Although their friendship continued over the years, it was not until the 1950s that Ralph Titshall mentioned his dilapidated shed full of old glass negative plates fused together by damp. He gave the plates to Doug to do what he would with them.

Doug began to take the negatives home, and he and his wife spent many a winter's night prising the glass plates apart, saving perhaps a third of them. He had no darkroom facilities and could only enjoy the pictures of his beloved Suffolk by holding them to the light. Although some of the pictures were printed over the years, they lay mainly untouched until Doug Cotton contacted me.

I decided I would tackle the task of printing each surviving picture, damaged or undamaged, believing that the images were too important to ignore just because of a few blemishes. The photographs had every exposure and contrast range you can imagine so that bringing them to life challenged all my 35 years' photographic experience.

Although photography was reasonably advanced in the 1920s, the Titshall brothers used a large wooden-and-brass stand camera focused through the back under a black cloth, with a technique going back to the Victorian period. Exposure was long, around half a second, and you can see movement in several of the pictures. Doug Cotton remembers them working with a shutterless camera. "They just used to take the bung (lens cap) off the front," he said.

Although I have worked with this fascinating photographic record for ten years, it remains a mystery to me why the Titshall brothers took what were everyday scenes in the 1920s.

Nobody is dressed in their best clothing or prepared for the camera, and although the pictures are clearly posed nobody then or now would photograph a road gang or a team of tree fellers and expect to see a commercial return. If the Titshalls took the pictures because they had the vision to see that it would all change forever as life became more mechanised, why did they discard them just a few years later?

The mysteries of the Titshall brothers will perhaps remain unsolved, but what is certain is that their work is a unique record of East Anglian rural life between the wars. Their pictures capture a way of life that was hard, with few comforts, when folk often lived their whole lives without leaving the county - or in some cases the village.

We owe a big thank you to the Titshall brothers and Doug Cotton, and I hope you will enjoy this glimpse of life from the 1920s and 30s.

David Kindred, 1999

Ralph Titshall standing outside 436 Spring Road, Ipswich

The Farming Scene

When the Titshall brothers took their photographs around Ipswich between 1925 and 1935, most local farms followed some variation of the Norfolk four-course rotation: roots - barley - seeds - wheat. The roots were originally turnips and swedes for animal feed, and on light soils these were eaten by sheep folded on them. The seeds were principally red clover with or without rye-grass, and peas, beans and potatoes were also popular crops. Some farms had dairy herds of perhaps fourteen cows, milked by hand for local consumption.

Compared with today, there were far more farms, and they were smaller; there were also a good number of smallholdings and farmed allotments. There were very few tractors. Farms revolved around horses and horsemen.

Wheat prices had a great effect on arable farm prosperity. In 1920, following government intervention in response to the wartime disruption of grain imports, the price of wheat was reasonably high. However, the protective Corn Production Act was repealed in 1921 and prices halved. Real disaster came in 1930-35 when prices fell to a quarter of their 1920 level.

Although some relief was provided by the sugar-beet subsidy from 1925, in general these photographs were taken at a time when arable farming fortunes were low and falling.

1. William Pendle and his three-year-old daughter with a prize Friesian cow from Hill Farm, Baylham, farmed by William Richards. Before a ban was instituted in 1880, Dutch cattle had been regularly imported into East Anglia. Imports were allowed again from 1914 and the British Friesian breed grew rapidly in popularity.

2. The same cow as above, with a different handler. Whereas standards of dairy farming were reportedly 'primitive' in the mid-1920s, British Friesians responded well to the good conditions of housing which became more common in the 30s.

3. The Red Poll cow was produced in the nineteenth century by breeding the small red Norfolk Horned beef breed with the Polled (i.e. hornless) Suffolk Dun, noted for its exceptional dairy qualities. The result was an outstanding dual-purpose animal, good for both beef and milk.

4. With its distinctive incurving horns and 'mealy' ring around the muzzle, the Jersey cow was prized for the butterfat content of its milk.

5. Sheep grazing stubble after the crop has been harvested and stacked. Although sheep were still important on Suffolk farms, they were soon to lose their place to sugar beet. Sheep production became a speciality of grassland farms in other parts of Britain.

6. Lux Farm, Playford, where Samuel Sherwood farmed in the mid-20s. The shepherd and his assistant are bottle-feeding orphan lambs. The Suffolk breed, with its distinctive black face and legs, was - and is - valued for its prolific breeding and abundant milk supply for lambs.

7. Shelter was provided by a temporary lambing yard built of straw and hurdles. Ted Taylor, shepherd at Willisham Hall Farm, remained day and night with his flock. The farmer, Malcolm Fiske, would have provided him with a hut and a stove.

8. Using a wooden twin-handled plough, the horseman appears to be working in traditional long stetches, about 16 feet wide, two widths of the drill. Drainage furrows at either side of the stetches jolted reaping machines out of action, and the days of stetch-work were numbered.

9. Single-furrow ploughing on light land with a pair of horses, the furrow horse with its hooves in the previous furrow, the land horse on the unploughed ground. Visible behind the ploughman is a hay feeder for sheep.

10. This single-handled wooden plough was probably a Ransomes AY, made in Ipswich from the early 1800s. The ploughman held on to a 'stalk' at the end of the handle so that he was able to control the horse with one hand and drive the plough with the other.

11. Ploughing continued right through the year. In both this photograph and the one above, the ploughmen are working in the summer on previously ploughed land. The horses' heads are decorated with elder leaves to keep flies away.

12. Ploughing very light land with one horse and a Ransomes single-furrow Pony plough with wheels.

13. More than enough work for a pair with a Ransomes YL plough, this heavy soil is being ploughed before the winter frosts which will break the clods down.

14. The land to the right of the photograph has been rolled immediately after ploughing. This could be in preparation for the sowing of winter wheat in the autumn, or it could be a springtime practice to conserve moisture.

15. In stetch-work the ploughtman made a number of parallel openings across the field and then ploughed round and round each opening until all the land was turned.

16. An unusual-looking group. The heavily bearded man in the centre is also to be seen in Plate 192.

17. On heavy land a ploughman could expect to plough about three-quarters of an acre a day. On lighter land he would complete the full acre, walking ten to eleven miles.

18. Just visible, the wide setting to the wheels on this plough indicates it is a two-furrow model - which would require a team of three horses.

19. Double-furrow plough, probably ploughing-in the clover stubble before wheat was sown.

20. This four-horse team are hitched to a Martin spring-tined cultivator to break down the hard clods on summer-ploughed or fallow land.

21. A multiple hitch, with four horses in front and up to another four behind. The implement is a heavy cultivator with a fore-carriage being used to break up land that has not been ploughed.

22. On hard, ploughed land the weight of two logs of wood is improving the effectiveness of a spike-toothed harrow, known locally as a heavy crab harrow.

23. The heavy cultivator looks identical to the implement shown in Plate 21. The large number of men, with more in the background, suggests that a practical demonstration was taking place.

24. The Ipswich sugar-beet factory opened at Sproughton in 1925, offering farmers a guaranteed income. Here a field of beet is being hoed for the last time before the leaves of the crop meet across the rows. The boy led the horse while his companion steered the hoe with the handles.

25. These A-hoes, set narrow, were probably being used to clear weeds between the rows of root crops such as turnips. Horse hoeing was regarded by many as monotonous work.

26. In Suffolk, horses were usually worked 'one journey', from early morning until mid afternoon, with a break for elevenses. The horseman's favoured riding position to and from work was on the nearside, or left.

27. Tractors were beginning to appear on farms. The Fordson Model F was one of the world's first mass-produced tractors, made in Ireland and America. This example, produced in Cork in about 1919-22, was fitted with optional long-wing mudguards.

28. This Model F Fordson was probably imported from the United States in 1925-6. The box on the side housed a trembler coil ignition. Altogether, some three-quarters of a million Model Fs were built worldwide from 1917 to 1928.

29. Pulling a Ransomes No. 3 Dauntless rigid-tine harrow, this International, probably a 10/20 manufactured in 1930-31, was becoming prized by progressive farmers for its sturdy construction and reliability.

30. The competition between the horse and the tractor continued right through the 1930s, with both sides claiming superiority. Unlike a horse, this International, seen ploughing, did not need to be fed when it was not working.

31. A two-horse flat roll, made by R. Hunt & Co., of Earls Colne being used to retain moisture on freshly ploughed land.

32. The one-horse flat roll was used to prepare a seed bed for root crops and then again after the crop had emerged as a control for flea-beetle. The implement was built in two sections so that the rolls could be placed one behind the other to negotiate gateways.

33. A two-horse Cambridge roll, sometimes used to put corrugations on the surface of the land before seed was broadcast. This reduced wind-blow on dry soil and prevented surface panning by rain.

34. Three horses (the middle one is mostly obscured), hitched to a drill for sowing seed, probably spring barley. The drill was almost certainly made by Smyth at Peasenhall in Suffolk.

35. The leading man controlled the horses with the reins, while steering the drill with a handle on the fore-carriage. His colleague put the drill in and out of gear on the headlands and kept an eye on the flow of seed to the coulters.

Haysel and Harvest

The Suffolk harvest began at the end of May with the cutting of the clover to make 'stover' for horse fodder. Haysel followed ('sel' comes from the Old English *sael*, meaning 'time' or 'season'), and then there was a break until the cereal harvest. Although horse-drawn harvesting implements had replaced the scythe and sickle, the work was still labour-intensive and demanding. Everyone lent a hand.

Other crops to be harvested included peas, beans and potatoes. Turnips were giving way to mangolds with their higher dry-matter content for animal feed. After some false starts, sugar beet was now becoming an acceptable industrial crop grown under contract for the new processing factory in Ipswich. Mangold and sugar beet roots can be distinguished from each other by their shapes: the former round, the latter long and tapering.

36. A pause during haymaking with a horse-drawn mower. Mowers needed frequent oiling to keep them operating at their working pace of 2½ miles an hour, and it was always advisable to have a spare knife available, with someone responsible for keeping it sharp.

37. Raking up and loading hay in what looks to be a new orchard. The wooden rakes would have been locally made, while the wide-tined pitchfork was a loose barley fork.

38. The sail reaper cut corn with a reciprocating blade. The revolving rakes or sails swept the corn to the knife and then cleared the platform, depositing the cut material in bundles for hand-tying to one side, away from the hooves of the horses in the next round.

39. Wheat was cut before it was dead ripe and formed into shocks, or stooks, of eight to twelve sheaves. The crop continued to ripen in the shocks for a week to a fortnight before it was loaded and carted to be built into stacks. The wagon was a factory-made 'boat wagon'.

40. Barley was often carted loose, rather than tied into sheaves. This traditional wagon belonged to Fred Smith, one of the principal landowners in Hasketon, with Church and Manor farms.

41. Stacks were carefully built for stability and to protect the crop against bad weather. The centre of the stack was supposed to be kept higher than the walls, so that the straws sloped downwards and outwards. Successive layers were placed to overlap at the edges, giving the stack its characteristic overhang.

42. Working in the rick yard, these men might be clearing up after building a stack, or preparing the base of a new one. A good stack had to be built on a dry bottom, which preferably allowed air to circulate below the crop.

43. During the winter the stacked corn had to be threshed so that the grain could be separated out and bagged. The threshing drum is on the extreme left of the photograph and leading across to the right is the elevator which conveyed straw to the new stack.

44. The threshed straw was later used for livestock bedding. The man on the right is wearing a muffler or 'wrapper' tied to one side around his neck; customarily this would have been red-spotted.

45. On the left are two thatched corn stacks; on the right a haystack partly cut down for feed. The high conical thatched roof of a good weatherproof corn stack can be clearly seen in the middle of the photograph.

46. This winter scene is probably of hay being loaded on to the wagon to be carted to the farmyard for winter feed. The man on the right is carrying the fruits of the dog's hunting along the stack bottom.

47. A potato-digging plough was used to loosen and lift the potato tubers. Bars slanting upwards and backwards were attached to the share to act like a sort of riddle, leaving most of the potatoes exposed while the soil fell back through the bars.

48. The potato spinner had revolving tines that threw the potatoes to one side of the row.

49. A pause in the potato harvest. The back-breaking task of collecting the loosened potatoes was carried out by women and children from the farm and village. The woman on the right of the standing row is wearing a cloth band round her neck, crossed over her chest and tied behind her waist, a style current a century before this photograph was taken.

50. The pea crop required careful harvesting if the peas were not to fall out of the pods, and some farmers preferred to use a pea-hook or hay-toppler rather than a grass-cutter. The crop was cut before it was ripe and then turned several times in the field.

51. Sugar-beet roots were loosened in the soil by a lifting plough, driven by the man on the left. The roots were then pulled by hand and knocked together to remove as much soil as possible. The sacks worn back to front offered protection from rain or wind when the men bent down to their work.

52. The topping gang used beet hooks to remove not just the leaves, but the whole of the beet 'crown'. The tops were used for cattle feed or in some instances left on the field and ploughed in as green manure.

53. The sugar beet in the tumbril could have been on its way to the railway yard where it was sent by rail direct to the processing factory. More probably it was joining a heap for later transport. General carting of this kind was a youngster's job.

54. In the late 1920s, seven tons of sugar beet was a typical yield per acre, a third of what would be expected today. Some of this crop at Hemingstone has been loaded on to the lorry in the background, ready for transport to the factory.

55. This tumbril cart, characterised by its large wheels, medium-high sides and rearward-tipping action, was the humbling execution vehicle of the French Revolution. Here it is loaded with mangolds.

56. Mangolds heaped in a clamp for winter stock feed.

57. Frost protection was provided for mangolds by covering their clamp with a thick layer of straw.

58. Mangolds were a popular feed for dairy cows because they caused no taint in the milk. However, if they were fed when freshly pulled they caused the animals to scour, so they needed to be stored until the end of December, during which time the cane sugar in the roots was converted to fructose and lactose. The cart belonged to the Eastern Counties Farmers Co-operative Association.

59. The hedging and ditching gang. The scythe is a Border model, with a shorter blade than was used for harvesting. It was ideal for the ends and corners of fields and for ditches.

60. Paused around the brazier for warmth. The fourth man from the left is also to be seen with some of his companions in plate 63.

61. Hedging and ditching.

62. The fire is just getting going, to offer comfort during a break. Several of the men have pipes on the go.

63. The oak has probably been felled by farm workers rather than woodsmen. There is no indication that a 'draw' has been cut to hinge the fall, and the tools look inappropriate.

64. All wearing collars and ties, this group are perhaps estate workers. The tumbril is loaded with even-length stakes, probably ash for turnery; the lettering on its side is indistinct.

Threshing and Steam Power

The threshing season started at the end of harvest and ran through to the following May. Although older workmen might have remembered using the flail, threshing was fully mechanised by the 1920s, with steam engines pulling and driving threshing drums.

The Ipswich area can claim a proud heritage in steam. At the Royal Show in 1841 Ransomes of Ipswich exhibited what is believed to have been the first portable steam engine, and the following year it was made self-moving - a traction engine travelling at 6 miles an hour. In 1856 the first steam ploughing outfit was produced for Ransomes by William Worby and tested near Ipswich at Nacton.

The photographs taken by the Titshalls show steam in its heyday. The up-and-coming competitor was of course the internal combustion engine, and by 1927 one of the great traction engine builders, Marshalls of Gainsborough, was turning away from steam and developing petrol- and diesel-powered tractors. In the 1940s the Field Marshall became the most popular machine for driving threshing drums, until combine harvesters in their turn made threshing drums obsolete.

65. On the road: Marshall No. 40101, a 6 hp compound traction engine built in November 1903 and owned by John and Arthur Barrell of Hall Farm and Bridge Farm, Coddenham. The engine is pulling a Clayton & Shuttleworth drum and an elevator. Suspended on the front of the engine are the spuds or cleats that would be fixed to the rear wheels to give extra grip.

66. Threshing sets would usually only be owned by the wealthier farmers or contractors. The owners provided two men, one of whom was the driver while the other fed the corn to the drum. The farmer had to provide the eight to ten more workers who were needed, as well as coal and water.

67. Carts made by the local blacksmith were used to supply water for steam engines and farm livestock. Ponds were dug shallow at one side so the horse and cart could back into the water. Standing on the frame, the workman bucketed water into the cart through two doors which opened on the top.

68. The tumbril in the foreground is being loaded with grain for carting. Farmers often had just one or two ricks or barns threshed at a time, so a contractor could make several visits over the long season. A water cart is to be seen in the right foreground.

69. A small engine, probably a Garrett, thought to belong to one of the Turner family at Hintlesham, and a small, early drum. The photograph shows a typical workforce, with the driver on the right and two men pitching sheaves from the corn stack to the man feeding the drum (centre background).

Two or three more are building the straw stack at the very back of the picture, beyond the elevator. At ground level, left, two men are clearing the chaff or cavings as they accumulate, and in the centre three others are loading sacks of grain. A youngster would be going to and fro driving the tumbril or fetching coal and water.

70. This 6 hp Burrell No.1679 single-crank compound engine was built in August 1893. Up to 1928 it was owned by Ernest Salmon who had Coddenham Green and Lime Kiln farms. It then passed to Percy Pallant of Wherstead, part of a large family farming at Valley Farm, Park Farm and Thorington Hall.

71. A windy day, with canvas rigging up to prevent sheaves blowing off the drum. Taken at Wherstead Hall farm in 1930. Standing from the right are 4-year-old Dennis Tucker, his father and George Steward who at the 1973 Suffolk Show was to be presented with a medal by the Duchess of Gloucester for completing 70 years work at Wherstead Hall. The driver is Mr Dunt.

72. Garretts of Leiston built both the threshing drum and the traction engine, a single-cylinder model No. 27318, made in September 1908 and owned by Walter Turner of Northlands Farm, Hintlesham, a principal landowner of the district. The thresher separated the grain, polished it and then graded it into two or three different sizes which were fed into separate sacks hanging from the pegs at the back of the drum. Handling the 18-stone wheat sacks was made easier by the hoist to the left of the picture.

73.

This engine, also shown on page 43, is a Marshall 6 hp built in 1912 and owned until 1928 by J.W. & A. Pearl, threshing contractors of Otley. The man in the centre is wearing out his First World War tunic; the man behind him has a stone beer or ginger beer flagon under his arm. The distinctive stack is held by hazel broaches rather than ties.

74. A Ransomes, Sims and Jefferies 7 hp single-cylinder engine No. 12738 built in 1899 and owned in 1925 by W.F. Paul, 'farmer and landowner, breeder of horses, Red Poll cattle and Suffolk sheep, Kirton Lodge, Corporation and Manor farms'. The full sack between the men on the ground was hired from Firmins of Ipswich (see Plates 144-5).

75. In the foreground is a water cart with its lid back. The rear wheel of the traction engine - probably a Ransomes - has been equipped with cleats for extra grip and the engine has a super heater.

76. Nothing was wasted during the threshing process. Short straws and leaves - cavings - often mixed with clover and grass leaves were separated out by the machine to be forked into sacks for animal feed. The husks of the grain - chaff - were bagged by the machine, also for animal feed.

77. With a canopy giving away its origins, this 5 hp Brown & May showmans tractor of 1912, No. 8643, was bought in 1928 by Dawson's of Rushmere (see also Plate 87). The driver was Jim Rackham.

78. Straw could be chopped in a chaff-cutter and mixed with other ingredients for animal feed. This chaff-cutter was made by C.H. Innes & Co. of Hitchin and owned by A. Harvey of 'Bilder Stone'. Cutting blades were attached to a flywheel and the speed could be adjusted to chop the material into different lengths.

79. The internal combustion engine began to challenge steam seriously from the First World War onwards. In what would otherwise be a traditional threshing scene, the power here is provided by an Overtime tractor imported from the USA, probably about 1917. The mudguards and seat have been removed for easier operation.

80. A petrol-driven stationary power unit of unknown make being used to power a threshing drum. The lettering on the sack reads 'North Eastern Railways 1926'. Later tractors could run a thresher all day on five gallons of diesel and they had enough power to haul the tackle just like a steam engine.

81. In the yard of Bloomfield's at Debenham, a Burrell 6 hp compound-cylinder traction engine No. 3925, owned by R.H. & R. Paul, one of the principal landowners at Sutton and Shottisham. It is hauling trailer wheels.

82. A Garrett 4CD engine, fitted with a canopy and Boulton blocks on the wheels for road work. The photograph was taken in about 1928 at Bloomfield's of Debenham. Left to right are: Charlie Clarke, Roy Bloomfield, Donald Martin, Malcolm Bloomfield.

83. Steam had also been applied to ploughing. Dating back to 1878, this 14 hp ploughing engine was owned by Charles Cherrington, blacksmith of Hadleigh, standing second from the right. Built by Fowler, No. 3497, the engine's original cylinder casting was replaced with a Burrell cylinder in 1923-4, turning it into a single-crank compound machine. Ploughing machines worked in pairs placed at opposite sides of large fields, hauling the plough by cable between them. The cable can be seen between the spokes of the nearest wheel; the paired engine is on the left of the photograph.

84. Built in October 1911 and fitted with an acetylene lighting system, this Foden No. 2782 4-ton steam wagon was owned by the Eagle Haulage Co., engineers, ironfounders and scale-makers of Rapier Street, Ipswich. The wagon was scrapped in 1928.

85. Photographed in 1926 at the Four Sisters junction, East Bergholt, this road roller is a 6-ton Type BLD Aveling & Porter No. 9095. It was built in 1920 and owned by East Suffolk County Council, Fleet No. 2. The foreman on the right is Stanley Pipe of Grundisburgh; the driver was Charles Wiffen, and the boy has been claimed to be Bill Southgate or Archibald Last. Their living van is behind the roller and they have a kettle on the fire.

86. A road-making gang.

87.

'Ruby', a Ruston Proctor 11-ton Type SR roller No. 43831, built in 1912. It was operated by the Rushmere St Andrew company, Alfred Dawson & Co., contractors for steam ploughing, road rolling, haulage and threshing, and general engineers.

88. This road gang are working with a 10-ton Garrett No. 34085 roller, built 1921-2. It was operated by East Suffolk County Council, Fleet No. 4. Steam rollers were first developed in 1865 by Thomas Aveling, and they were produced up to 1946.

89. An example of the type of portable steam engine developed in the middle of the nineteenth century, and thought to be a Marshall. The engine had to be hauled from place to place by horse or another vehicle. It is driving a saw bench. At the front of the engine is a winch to help pull the timber on to the blade.

Horses and Horsemen

Although horses had been used on British farms along with oxen for a thousand years, the great era of the horse began in the nineteenth century. Improved agricultural techniques and a more intensive use of the land resulted in a greater number of ploughings and cultivations in the course of a year. Furthermore, new implements such as seed drills, fertiliser distributors and horse hoes meant that the horse increasingly supplemented or replaced hand labour.

Horses were also an important agricultural product in their own right, bred on the farm for sale to customers needing animals for drays, delivery carts and omnibuses, or for carriage and riding horses. Before the First World War there were over a million 'agricultural' horses in Britain, and even in 1921 there were 962,000 - reflecting both on-farm and off-farm uses. By the Second World War this number had fallen to 650,000.

When the Titshall brothers recorded these scenes in the 1920s and 30s, the use of working horses was only just past its peak.

90. In some places the conventions of the nineteenth century persisted past the First World War and into the 1920s - for instance, the strict precedence of the head horseman and the hierarchy below him, always going out and coming back in their proper places.

91. Horses were kept out at pasture from early spring until as late in the year as conditions allowed.

92. On Suffolk farms a horseman's day began at 4 a.m. when after a bite of bread and cheese he hurried to the stables to feed the horses. They were turned out for ploughing at 6.30 - 7.00 a.m. and worked, with breaks, until 2.30 in the afternoon. The horseman fed his animals and had his own dinner at about 3 o'clock, after which he returned to groom the horses, finishing at about 5.30 p.m.

93. Larger farms might have five or six specialist horsemen. On smaller farms a labourer might be expected to turn his hand to any task, horse work included. The saddle of this horse is well-padded to take the weight of the shafts.

94. Carting in muddy conditions. The horseman's day was not complete until he had removed all the mud from the horses' hooves and legs. "A horse is only as good as its legs" was a popular saying.

95. Although horse work on the farm reached a peak with autumn ploughing, there were jobs to be done most of the year, and usually horsemen were not laid off like other labourers when work was slack.

96. A second or trace horse could be used for heavy loads, with the larger horse usually at the front. Normally the pair were driven by a single horseman who walked at the head of the rear horse and drove the front horse by means of light touches on a continuous rein.

97. The Titshall photographs of horsemen show a variety of dress, reflecting the social changes of the 1920s. Many are wearing knee straps, called Yorkies, 'lijahs or lanigens, which prevented trousers dragging on the knees.

98. It was uncommon for a horseman to take a whip to work like the one being held here in the horseman's left hand. Perhaps he had been breaking in a young horse, having it pull a log of wood. Horses were usually fully trained by the age of four or five, and on some farms a horseman received an extra payment for completing the training successfully.

99. "I was born on a Suffolk farm; and when I was a boy I used to lie in bed in the early morning and listen to the quiet champing of the horses, the clink of their shoes on the cobbles of the stables, and the horsemen whistling or hissing through their teeth to soothe the horses as they brushed or curry-combed them before turning out." Quoted in *The Horse in the Furrow* by George Ewart Evans.

100. In arable areas with an abundance of straw, horses were sometimes kept in straw-filled yards rather than at pasture or in steamy stables. The stable area was the centre of activity on the farm.

101. Each horseman usually had his own horses to look after and care for, though there had to be some flexibility and co-operation to fit the changing demands of the farming year. Ploughboys looked forward to the time when they too could have their own team.

102. True-bred Suffolk horses, the one on the left dappled. The Suffolk was small for a working horse, with the barrel chest that helped earn its name of Punch. It was sorrel or one of seven shades of chestnut in colour; the star on the forehead or the 'shim' (blaze) down the face was a common - if not always approved - feature.

103. "Poverty in the stable soon reached the house." Working horses were usually fed one and a half to two bushels (63-84 lb.) of oats a week, though many owners kept the allowance down to one bushel. Other feeds included hay and straw, as well as beans, maize, bran and roots.

104. Sacks were worn to save the men's knees when they were hauling bags about.

105. The boy is wearing a Salvation Army cap and cycle clips. His bicycle wheel is just visible between the spokes of the nearest cart wheel.

106. On his legs the horseman is wearing puttees, no doubt from the First World War. The plates on the tumbril are unclear.

107. Carters used horses of a wide range of conformations and types.

108. Strong, steady and persevering, the Suffolk Punch was almost purely a farm horse. Its large 'bread basket' allowed it to work one shift, rather than taking the long midday feed break usual in other parts of the country. This horse was probably bred from a Suffolk stallion and a Shire mare.

109. Children became familiar with horses almost from birth. They might start work at twelve or thirteen, but they would usually be eighteen or so before they were ready to start ploughing. The beginner would plough behind the head man and ahead of another experienced horseman, so that his mistakes would be covered up.

110. In view of its swollen knees and ankles, it is tempting to believe that this is an old pony that had done a lot of road work with a trap. Horses would be expected to work until between sixteen and twenty years of age.

111. The woman's cloche felt hat, long coat, blouse and skirt are typical of the 1920s, while the childrens' clothes could have placed them at any time from 1920 to 1940. Slight differences in their clothing suggest that the left-hand child was a boy, and the right-hand one a girl.

112. A tub cart, the slightly less elegant version of the governess car designed to be used to transport children safely along country lanes and estate roads. It had an awkward, sideways-on driving position. The woman's straw boater and waisted dress with a very full skirt are fashions belonging more to 1900-1910 than the 1920s.

113. Pausing on his round, the butcher with his striped apron and neatly turned-out horse and cart.

114. At the show: the nearer horse has a prize rosette on its bridle. Brown & Woods, The Priory, Wolsey Street, Ipswich, were manufacturers of horticultural requisites.

115. Fitted with a lamp for night driving, this is perhaps a dealer's cart, ready for market.

116. Weavers were carters of Schreiber Road, Ipswich; one of their trucks is shown in Plate 142. With a brass on its forehead and shining brass hames around its collar, the horse looks as though it has been dressed up for something special.

Trades and Transport

The Titshall brothers were interested in people at all kinds of work. They mined a rich vein of trades and skills, much of which was in some way dependent on agriculture, even if it was in an urban setting.

117. Operating from the Woodbridge Road, Ipswich, W. Wakeling styled themselves haulage contractors and general carters. They were used by large companies such as Ransomes, Sims and Jefferies, as well as for smaller jobs.

118. A heavy delivery wagon, owned by the rick cloth and tentmakers, Rands & Jeckell of Old Foundry Road and Gt Coleman Street, Ipswich, dressed up for a show.

119. Felixstowe Urban District Council dustmen John Cross (left) and Mr Pettit, both of Walton, photographed at Grange Road, Felixstowe.

120. On the bank behind this Dennis lorry is a load of sugar beet, probably about to be transported to the factory. The left-hand man is holding a beet fork and the lorry's side extensions have been put up to increase capacity.

121. The start of the Soames coach businesss, now run from Otley and Woodbridge. In 1925 Albert Soames (centre) was listed as 'a hawker'. His first van, bought in 1924, was this Talbot, which he operated out of Clopton, selling a wide range of goods, including paraffin at 4d (less than 2p) a gallon. George Button (right) helped, while the man to the left was Almer Steel, an Otley butcher.

122. John Freston's 1930 registration, 1½-ton maroon Chevrolet is loaded with hay trusses. Each one would have been cut 3ft by 2 ft from the stack with a broad-bladed hay knife and might then have been compacted in a press. Frestons were hay, straw and corn merchants.

123. The Orwell Park Dairies milkman was William ('Bill') Keeble, who delivered to the village of Nacton. It is thought that the shot was taken at the corner known locally as Post Office Hill. The milk was carried from the churn in a can to the customer's doorstep - or tradesman's entrance - where it was measured out into a jug.

124. North of Ipswich, outside the moated church of Culpho with its unbuttressed tower south of the nave, about 1928-30. The driver of the Morris Commercial van was Thomas Pleasance, his delivery boy Eric Borley. Alnesbourne Dairies and Bakeries had premises in the Norwich Road, Ipswich as well as the Felixstowe Road.

125. Ernest Rush ran his dairy from Chilton Hall Farm, Bury Road, Stowmarket. With its cranked axle, the dairy float was specially designed for low-loading. In some of these carts a system of rings and pivots, called gimbals, kept the churns steady to reduce the souring of the milk.

126. 'Town horses were nearly always leg-weary. They often did up to forty miles on the road during the day, and they got in the habit of sliding and dragging their feet. They just burned their shoes up.' Suffolk blacksmith Clifford Race, quoted by George Ewart Evans in *The Horse in the Furrow.*

127. The Sycamore Dairy was run from Sycamore House Farm, Bramford by Geo. Jackson. This picture is believed to have been taken at the Bramford Show.

128. A style of vehicle typically used as a bakery van from the end of the Victorian era, but increasingly superseded by motor vans or electric trucks in the 1930s. Here, Walter Wright is delivering milk at Brantham; Braham Hall was owned by a Mrs Portway in the late 1920s.

129. A strongly made, plain wagon outside the Customs House, Ipswich Dock. The large stitched sacks might have contained malt.

130. An Albion lorry belonging to Livermore's haulage contractors, loaded with R & W Paul's sacks, at Ipswich Dock. Among Paul's brands was 'Kositos', cooked and flaked maize for dairy cow feed. Kositos was promoted as being bulky, palatable and containing minerals for vigorous health and growth - little wonder that it was also reportedly used as a human breakfast cereal.

131. Unloading at Ipswich Dock - perhaps wheat or maize meal. Before the First World War cheap grain imports had devastated British cereal farming, leaving the country vulnerable when its shipping was attacked. With the ending of protection in 1921, imports again began flooding in.

132. Loading a Thames barge at the New Cut, Ipswich.

133. A coal-fired tar boiler, probably built by John Yates, Birmingham, around 1900, close to the Lord Nelson public house, Ashbocking. The foreman, on the right of the road gang, was apparently known as 'Big Ollie'.

134. Building the sugar-beet factory at Sproughton, 1925, close to the old tare house and lime kiln. The gang mixed the concrete and raised the walls between the steel-work two feet at a time.

135. In 1925 there were still 25 brickmaking companies in Suffolk, with a particular concentration around Sudbury. However, that is far fewer than there had been twenty years earlier, and the hand brickmaker in his shelter was a vanishing breed.

136. Clay and sand were mixed into a 'pug' from which the green bricks were moulded in individual wooden moulds. To prevent damage before they were dried, the green bricks were turned out of the moulds on to the pallets seen stacked in the foreground.

137. The green bricks were stacked in 'hacks': long rows, protected from sun and rain by boarded roofs. Here, dried bricks are being carted from the hacks to the kiln for firing.

138. Brickworks made a range of products such as the pipe being held by the man standing third from the right. The workmen are posed in front of the kiln; standing third from the left is the brickmaker in Plate 136.

139. The Model T Ford, with its solid rear tyres, was owned by E. Saunders of Dovercourt, builder and contractor.

140. Loading fired bricks to supply orders.

141. A tumbril-load of industrially produced bricks, with sharp, regular edges. The long tradition of locally produced bricks was coming to a close.

142. 86-year-old Doug Cotton, who saved the Titshall photographs, remembers that he used to see this cream-and-brown Fordson truck, registered 1934, 'nearly every day'. The vehicle was owned by Weavers (see Plate 116), who are collecting sand from Tuddenham sandpit. The full container at the end of the rail is about to be tipped forward to load the contents into the lorry.

143. Gate hurdles for temporary sheep pens had to be robust, but at the same time light and portable. In East Anglia ash was usually used, from the same coppices that supplied rakes and scythe handles. The hurdle-maker was working at Bucklesham Mill, on the Mill River between Kirton and Newbourne. Although the three-storey building still stands, the house was demolished to make way for an experimental water desalination plant.

144. Before the advent of plastic bags, sacks were vital to cereal farming and other industries, and there was a national sytem of sack hiring, delivery and recovery. This is the warehouse of Firmin & Co., Handford Road, Ipswich.

145. A Thomas Firmin was recorded as a sackmaker in Essex in 1785, moving to Ipswich in the mid nineteenth century. Besides sacks, the company made all kinds of canvas goods including rick cloths; they wove coconut fibre into matting, span their own twine and made rope.

The straight lines of the women's clothing, their little ankle-strap shoes and hats worn low, as well as their hairstyles were all fashions of the 1920s.

146. George Reeve standing in the door of the Grundisburgh Saddler's Cottage. Saddlers and harness-makers had varied work which included all the horse gear, cart-trace harness and plough harness seen in earlier photographs. They adapted to changes in agriculture by turning their hands to webbing and straps for agricultural machinery.

147. A horse with good feet was reckoned to take about an hour to shoe, with the horseman or owner holding the animal quiet. The tools were a hammer, a pair of nippers, a rasp and an unclencher for taking off the old shoe. The tripod in the centre was a foot rest for the animal while its foot was being rasped. Uncharacteristically, this farrier is not wearing a smith's leather apron.

148. At Brockford Street, George Woodward stands with his sons, Ephraim and Victor, beneath a fine long-straw thatched roof. Harness-makers were largely dependent on farmers for their livings, and when harvests or prices were poor, they could expect slow payment This was another trade that was about to be devastated by the internal combustion engine.

149. Two wagon hubs are lying on the heap to the left of this picture and in the background there are several metal tyres, so this is almost certainly a wheelwright's or smith's yard.

150. Believed to have been taken in about 1925 at Bruisyard. Standing, left to right, are Archibald, Arthur and Stanley Clow. A smith's day could start at six in the morning and continue until six in the evening. One of the most gruelling jobs was making or re-sharpening the bills used by millers to dress their stones. 'A day of this shook you up and jarred your arms and shoulders so next day you could hardly raise your arm high enough to put your cap on.' Clifford Race, quoted in *The Horse in the Furrow.*

151. This photograph indicates some of the range of the smith's work, which was often combined with a wheelwright's. Jennings and Martin had their forge at Ash Street, Semer where Walter Martin (centre) continued working until his late 70s.

152. At Coddenham: the horse's owner on the left, then Mrs Offord, Mr Ethelred 'Ted' Offord and Percy Offord. Smithies were reckoned to be one of the centres of village life, and forges would often be thronged with gossiping neighbours. Smiths were also valued as judges of horses, a would-be purchaser being wise to seek their advice before buying a local animal.

153. This small coal-fired roller mill was built in the 1890s adjacent to one of the finest Suffolk windmills, at Swilland. The owner, Colonel C.A. Barron, is seated on the right of the group in the foreground; next to him is his 'butler'. Behind his head is a horse-drawn wagon, next to two Ford vans, registered 1924. To their right, the 1913 3-ton Foden steam wagon No. 4750 was owned by Barron's from 1925 to 1927. Eric Ruffles is standing in the left-hand doorway, and from him a gangplank leads leftwards to the windmill. The roller mill ceased production in the 1930s; it is now a pottery. Of the windmill only the base remains.

154.
The men in the doorway are covered in white flour from their work at this unknown miller's.

155. Thorington Street watermill and miller's house, near Stoke-by-Nayland, part of the Tendring Hall estate. Joseph Munson, miller until he died in 1933, is standing with his daughter Joyce who was born in 1922. Joseph was succeeded by his son Joe who retired when the mill ceased production in 1963. Dating back to 1760 on an earlier Domesday Book site, the mill has been preserved and is now in working order again.

156. A pause in what was no doubt a long day.

Village People

In the 1920s villagers were still suffering from the bereavements of the First World War and they also faced a renewed agricultural depression. Towns were becoming increasingly dominant, as indicated by the population figures given on page 126, and villages that were close to towns were also tending to grow, while smaller, more remote ones were declining.

Each village embraced people of a wide variety of personal circumstances, including poor widows, insecure labourers, apparently more secure horsemen, rural tradesmen, smallholders, farmers of acreages large and small, professionals and landowners. Some evidence of contrasts in personal fortune has been captured in the Titshalls' photographs, not only in the faces, demeanours and dress of their subjects, but also in the buildings that were their backdrops.

Many of the buildings date back to the seventeenth century, or even earlier, an indication of the continuity of the village. However, over the course of their lives the cottages and houses had usually been adapted to new uses with additions and subdivisions as well as external cladding and new doors and windows.

157. Everything about this man speaks of a lifetime of hard physical work.

158.

Wearing clothes more typical of 1912-14 than the mid-1920s, the women are standing in front of a timber-framed lobby-entrance house with a parlour and kitchen either side of the fireplace. The walls have been rendered in pebble-dash. The steep pitch of the roof suggests it was originally thatched. Above the gutter the pantiles are completed by a line of slates. The windows have wrought-iron opening lights set in wooden frames, protected by external shutters.

159. Nellie and Kathlene Pearl, about 1928, near the Fox Inn at Barking Tye (the Tye is a common of about 50 acres). Behind the right-hand woman's head can be seen vertical strips of the original wattle-and-daub panelling. Over this, horizontal oak laths were nailed to the timber frame and then covered in lime plaster. Above the horse's back is brick nogging infill which replaced some of the wattle-and-daub, probably in the eighteenth century, and all the indications are that this house originally dates back to the sixteenth century. There is a fine wide-plank door at the left of the house.

160. Ethel Gooding (left) and Jane Ramsay collecting firewood at Martlesham.

161. A nineteenth-century cottage, timber-framed and rendered. The pantiles on the shallow-pitched roof were originally introduced from Holland, sometimes arriving as ships' ballast.

162. The women are possibly stonepickers, wearing hessian aprons. They are standing in front of a house that is more substantial than many, with its railings, well-kept long-straw thatch, diamond quarries in the leaded lights in the upstairs window and rectangular leaded panes below. The doorway has a nice cased door with a debased classical influence extending to the brackets under the overhanging pentice board. Timber-framed and plastered, the house probably dates back to the seventeenth century.

163. The pump is protected from the frost by straw wrapped in sacking. The building is solidly constructed with Flemish-bond brickwork. The roof behind the women's heads is covered with locally produced plain tiles, while projecting in from the right is a corner covered with fish-scale pattern slates brought in by railway from Wales.

164. The substantial house to the right of the photograph has been added to and the extension then subdivided into two small cottages. Larger houses quite commonly had wells close at hand.

165. Although all the casement windows of the houses are nineteenth-century softwood-framed, signs of decorative patterning under the eaves show seventeenth- or eighteenth-century origins. The irregular windows and dormers suggest that this was a large house which was subdivided and had its dormers added.

166. Mr and Mrs George Leeks, Miss Nellie Cady (back) and Mrs Hills at 2, The Terrace, Lower Layham, about 1930.

167. Photographed in the mid-20s, Mr and Mrs Henry Southernwood of Lower Walton, Felixstowe who were to celebrate their 67th wedding anniversary in 1942. Henry worked as a shepherd until his employer stopped keeping sheep when he turned to general farm work such as hedging.

168. This couple's home might have been a purpose-built estate cottage. It was probably built in the nineteenth century, a mixture of random flint and brick. The brick quoins around the door and the round arches above it indicate a high quality of workmanship.

169. Believed to have been photographed at Coddenham, the walls of this family's timber-framed house are decorated with ropework or 'cable' patterning, just visible at the top of the photograph. This twisted, plaited pattern which was made with a comb in the wet plaster, was a decorative feature that persisted from the seventeenth century until the early twentieth.

170. Some of the details of this early nineteenth-century brick house suggest that it was of high-quality construction. For instance, above the windows the arches are made of rubbed, splayed (i.e. shaped) bricks, and below the eaves is a brick 'dentil' course. The substantial cast-iron guttering and softwood casement windows have been maintained in good condition.

171. A popular baconer, the 'blue-and-white pig' was a cross between a Large Black sow and a Large White boar.

172. With their ducks and assorted breeds of chickens, these women are standing in a farmyard dating back to the sixteenth or seventeenth century. Above their heads is a large grain barn, the oldest structure on the site, timber-framed and clad with feather-edge weather boarding. The smaller buildings around have been added at later periods. Three roofing materials are evident: traditional plain tiles, Dutch pantiles and Welsh slate.

173. Lucy Lambert, at Raydon, near the station. In the row of timber-framed cottages one of the doorways has been closed up. Timber-framed buildings were particularly adaptable to changing needs.

174. Feeding her ducks and ducklings, this woman is standing in front of a fine, classically inspired house perhaps built in the period 1830-40. The brickwork is probably of Suffolk white bricks and there are decorated brackets over the doorcase. The sash windows have delicate glazing bars with wooden lintels simulating stone. Altogether a house of quality.

175. A Suffolk shepherd with the tools of his trade – a leg crook and a collie dog.

176. Clinker Clarke at Grundisburgh Corner, with his daughter and granddaughter, about 1928. Their house is one of a row of nineteenth-century brick cottages with iron ties showing structural problems, perhaps due to the alterations suggested by the variations in brickwork.

177. A wintry village scene in which the group are standing in front of a sixteenth- or seventeenth-century timber-framed and plastered house which has probably been subdivided and changed over the centuries. The windows are shuttered and the door in the centre of the picture is a 'stable door' with independently opening top and bottom halves.

178. Various unsubstantiated legends – including links to the Napoleonic wars – are associated with Stone Cottage, Lower Street, Gt. Bealings. The front of the house is faced with coursed kidney flints into which dark blue glass bottle ends have been inserted for decoration. The woman's clothing is typical of the early 1930s.

179. This woman's mourning wear and hat reflect the Edwardian period, twenty years before this photograph was taken. Her shawl is as much for warmth as for decoration.

180. With a chimneystack dating back to the seventeenth century, this timber-framed house with its later dormer window could once have been a farmhouse of quality.

181. These are perhaps estate cottages, and there are signs that the Flemish-bond construction of local bricks is concealing something older behind it. To the left of the main house is an added washhouse or bakehouse with its own chimneystack.

182. Cecil Hood and his aunt, Ida Robinson, outside the cottage of Cecil's grandparents, George and Priscilla Hood, at Henley, in the late 1920s. Their cottage - now demolished - was of timber frame covered with plaster and decorated in panels. New softwood windows had replaced the originals, and the steep-pitched roof would once have been thatched. There was a large pentice board on the gable with weather boarding above, covering this most exposed part of the building.

183. Mr and Mrs William Blake of Ford's Green, Bacton, now called The Forge. William Blake was a thatcher.

184. New Hall Farm, Pettaugh. On the left are Winifred Brown, Grandmother and Alice Maude Brown. In 1929 an Arthur Brown was listed as farm bailiff to Pettaugh farmer Jas. Cutting. The main building (behind the man's head) is a cart lodge with a granary or hayloft on the upper floor, probably dating back to the eighteenth century. The other buildings are more recent, and all have been well maintained.

185. The woman on the right is wearing a dress with the straight lines and skirt length of the mid-1920s. Her female companion is perhaps a domestic servant, permitted to wear a dress of only a fuller length.

186. About 1928, Town House, Cotton (opposite Cotton Church), a pair of timber-framed, lime-plastered cottages with large overhanging thatch, now demolished. The group captures family life in the 1920s. On the left is Tom Alexander who was born in 1920 and grew up in Cotton where he still lives. With Tom is his mother Ethel (holding the baby, back row) and his four brothers and sisters between his mother and his grandparents. His parents and grandparents shared the cottages.

187. Wearing jodhpurs and a knitted pullover, this unknown man is a classic middle-class figure of the 1930s - not unlike the portrait of Ralph Titshall on Page 5.

188. A shooting party with beaters.

189. The man's suit has high lapels and straight trousers; the woman's dress is quite high-waisted and full at the back. The couple's clothing and bearing speak of the Edwardian age that had passed with the First World War.

190. Farmers, gamekeepers, villagers - many were familiar with the use of shotguns to supplement their diets with rabbits and pigeons or to control crop predators.

191. The district nurse at Somersham. Children were normally born at home and sick people were more often cared for at home than was to be the case after the Second World War.

192. It is plausible to believe that the brickwork of the hip-roofed house to the right of the picture conceals a medieval timber-framed house. The roof is just the right shape, with a tiny gablet at the end of the ridge through which smoke from the open fire could have escaped, until the large chimney stack in the top right of the picture was built. The downstairs windows were made in the nineteenth century and the dormer was also a later addition. The slate-roofed building to the left was added in the nineteenth century at the service end of the building - perhaps a dairy that became a shop. The man is also to be seen in Plate 16, wielding a big stick.

Names of Places

	Plate references	Population figures* 1911	1931
Ashbocking	133	279	241
Bacton	183	590	541
Barking	159	447	425
Baylham	1	258	249
Bildeston	78	729	618
Bramford	127	1,281	2,197
Brantham	128	989	1,033
Brockford	148	822[1]	801
Bruisyard	150	243	181
Bucklesham	143, page 4	264	232
Clopton	121	325	272
Coddenham	65, 70, 152, 169	647	656
Cotton	186	389	366
Culpho	124	87	79
Debenham	81, 82	1,196	1,016
East Bergholt	85	1,512	1,474
Felixstowe	119, 167	8.686	12,067
Grundisburgh	146, 176	743	756
Gt Bealings	178	302	270
Hadleigh	83	3,200	2,951
Hasketon	40	468	439
Hemingstone	54	249	222
Henley	182	243	237
Hintlesham	69, 72	561	559
Ipswich	84, 114, 116 - 18, 122, 129 - 32, 144, 145	73,932	87,569
Kirton	74, page 4	500	469
Layham	166	448	372
Martlesham	160	442	975
Nacton	123	455	483
Otley	73	523	518
Pettaugh	184	186	200
Playford	6	230	212
Raydon	173	492	435
Rushmere St Andrew	77, 87	463	1,133
Semer	151	290	178
Somersham	191	340	347
Sproughton	134	680	794
Stowmarket	125	4,230	6,428
Swilland	153	184	185
Stoke-by-Nayland	155	880	790
Tuddenham St Martin	142	362	310
Wherstead	70, 71	315	460
Willisham	7	141	119

* Figures extracted from *Kelly's Directories*

1 The population figure is for Wetheringsett-cum-Brockford; Brockford was a hamlet of Wetheringsett.

Other titles from Old Pond Publishing

Ferguson Tractors, *Stuart Gibbard.*
65-minute video showing forty models from the Ferguson Brown to the FE 35.

Ford Tractor Story Part 1: 1917-64. Part 2: 1964 to Today, *Stuart Gibbard.*
Highly illustrated, large-format hardback guides to the machines and the men who made them.

Harry Ferguson: inventor and pioneer, *Colin Fraser.*
The classic account of the great man's life and work in paperback.

Harvest from Sickle to Satellite, *Brian Bell.*
40-minute video history of combine harvesters and their predecessors.

Power of the Past, *Brian Bell.*
60-minute video capturing Britain's premier vintage working machinery event.

For more details or a catalogue please contact

Old Pond Publishing, 104 Valley Road, Ipswich IP1 4PA, United Kingdom.
Phone/fax +44 (0)1473 210176. Email r.smith@virgin.net

Acknowledgements

Some of the photographs in this book have previously been published in the *East Anglian Daily Times* and the *Evening Star* where they have awakened the memories of readers, often relatives of the people shown in the pictures. Their responses, filed by David Kindred and Doug Cotton, form the basis of many of the captions.

In addition, experts on particular aspects of the photographs have given up their time to suggest interpretations. Brian Bell and Fred Dyer gave invaluable guidance on the farming and harvesting chapters; Doug Cotton, Fred Dyer and Robin Harding helped with steam, while Tony Brown, the Road Locomotive Society Records Officer, was able to identify many of the engines. A retired horseman, Ernie Smith, aided by his wife Margaret, suggested captions for the working horse photographs and Michael Munt, Conservation Officer for the Mid-Suffolk District Council, gave interpretations of the buildings in the final chapter. Mark Barnard and Peter Dolman of the Suffolk Mills Group, Pam Crossley, Textile Assistant at the Manor House Museum, Bury St. Edmunds, Brian Dyes, Chairman of the Ipswich Transport Museum, tractor authority Stuart Gibbard and woodlands manager Andrew Moore all gave help in their areas of expertise. I must thank all these people for giving up their time so willingly.

I am also grateful for help given by Ivy and Jonathan Bell, Ken Goward, Sally Looker, Pansy Munson, Valerie Porter, Mary and Philip Ryder-Davies, Adam Smith (Museum of East Anglian Rural Life) and Lesley and Peter Smith. Brian Bell reviewed the text and Julanne Arnold kindly edited it.

Our knowledge of the Titshalls themselves has been provided by Doug Cotton, Vic and Beverley Lowne, Yvonne Titshall and George Turner. We are grateful for George Turner's permission to reproduce family photographs in the Introduction.

I have also sought the help of written sources. The Suffolk Record Office, Ipswich, contains directories of the period, some of the vehicle registration records, an excellent library and friendly staff.

The work of Jonathan Brown of the Museum of English Rural Life, Reading was extremely helpful on horses, as were books by George Ewart Evans. I am grateful to Faber and Faber Ltd., for permission to print extracts from *The Horse in the Furrow.*

I must apologise in advance for any errors and omissions; occasionally limitations of space have prevented my listing all the names of the subjects of the photographs.

It has been a privilege to work with these pictures and I am aware that much remains to be found out about them. We would be delighted to receive comments (which can be sent to Old Pond Publishing) giving further information about any of the photographs - or, indeed, the photographers.

Roger Smith

April 1999

Bibliography

Blythe, Ronald, *Akenfield* (Allen Lane, 1969)

Brown, Jonathan, *The Horse in Husbandry* (Farming Press, 1991)

Evans, George Ewart, *The Farm and the Village* (Faber and Faber, 1974)

Evans, George Ewart, *The Horse in the Furrow* (Faber and Faber, 1967)

Fream, W., ed. R.H. Biffen, *Elements of Agriculture 12th edn* (John Murray, 1932)

Johnson, B., *Steam Traction Engines, Wagons and Rollers* (Blandford Press, 1971)

Kelly's Directories of Ipswich & District, as well as Suffolk

Malster, Robert, *Suffolk at Work: trades and industries* (Sutton Publishing, 1996)

Newby, Howard, *Country Life: a social history of rural England* (Sphere Books, 1988)

Smith, D.J., *Discovering Horse-Drawn Farm Machinery 2nd edn* (Shire Publications, 1984)

Smith, D.J., *Discovering Horse-Drawn Vehicles* (Shire Publications, 1994)

Stratton, J.M., *Agricultural Records AD220 - 1968* (John Baker, 1969)

Trist, P.J.O., *A Survey of the Agriculture of Suffolk* (R.A.S.E., 1971)

Whitlock, Ralph, *A Short History of Farming* (EP Publishing, 1977)

Zeuner, Diana, ed., *The Working Horse Manual* (Farming Press, 1998)